BUII WEALTH THROUGH REAL ESTATE

BARRY SHARIF

BUILDING
WEALTH
THROUGH
REAL
ESTATE

BARRY SHARIF

Foreword by Nicole Horsch, author
of *Sermon on the Mount of Messy*

Acknowledgements

First and foremost, I want to thank God. Without God, I am nothing. Whatever I have accomplished in my life is through His grace. He is the One who gives and makes you shine, and He is the One who takes it away to make you humble. So, I give Him my gratitude, the glory, and the honor.

~

Next, I want to thank all the following people:

My children, Nestor, Jamal, Jasmine, Hayley, and Brandon. Thank you for being respectful, responsible, hardworking, and kind. You make me so proud.

~

My parents who instilled the value of hard work in me. They taught me to be kind and to always help others.

~

My bosses and mentors, Don King, Kirk Langs, Steve Blood, and Scott McGregor for grooming me, pushing me, and helping me to be a better leader to my team. You taught me what to do and most importantly, what not to do. You helped shape my career.

~

Mike Rakeman and Brian Schiele for being the most teachable college graduates who absorbed every bit of knowledge I taught them and put it to practice. They were the most loyal apprentices, protégés, and friends, and are now leading their own team and running their company. I am so proud of the men you have become.

Dan Milea, you are by far the most loyal friend and confidant. We may go weeks or months without talking, but when we do, I know that I can tell you anything and I know that you always have my back.

~

Nicole Horsch and Janice George for giving me tips on how to publish my book. Special thanks to Joanna Sanders (my editor for this publication, and author of *Fire Women*) for her expertise, advice, and help. Without you, this would not have been possible and may not have happened as fast as it did! You are amazing!

~

Most importantly, I want to thank my wife, Arline. You are my rock. You are there with me through thick and thin, you support me, you pray for me, you never judge me, you always smile, and bring joy into my life, and for that, I love you with all my heart!

Barry

BUILDING WEALTH
THROUGH REAL ESTATE

CONTENTS

Foreword

I remember my first phone call with Barry. It was about seven years ago. I was sitting at my daughter's swim lesson, and he called me after I sent an inquiry about refinancing our mortgage. We were deeply in debt and needed a lot of help. Interest rates had dropped considerably, and our home had increased in value, but our credit was not stellar at the time. I was nervous and quite frankly, embarrassed because our situation was not great. Many of the reasons for the debt were out of our control but no matter how hard we tried, we couldn't climb out of that dark pit ourselves. We needed help.

Barry was genuinely kind and friendly. There wasn't one ounce of judgement as I told our story. He listened and immediately offered me solutions. His solutions gave me hope! I remember leaving that swimming lesson excited to tell my husband that we could turn things around and we were going to have a plan to do it. Barry helped us refinance, pay off debt, and get rid of pesky mortgage insurance. He gave us step-by-step instructions and we followed that plan.

In a few short months, we were debt free except for our mortgage payment! A massive burden was lifted from us, and we could begin to dream about the future and possibilities. We believed we could help our kids pay for college and felt confident about providing for their futures.

Over the years, Barry helped us with another refinance, and we have referred friends to him who received the same kind of outstanding service. Recently, Barry worked with us for over a year as we built a home in a new city. We had wanted to move for a long time and a new job offer made this dream a possibility. Barry worked with us to secure an interest rate even when rates began to skyrocket, and our build was delayed repeatedly. He was the calm in a stormy situation. Barry would call us to give us a heads-up about the market and help us strategize appropriately. Sometimes he would just listen to us vent about the situation. Building a home in a post-pandemic world is not for the faint of heart!

We were able to close on our beautiful dream home with an interest rate far below the going rate because of Barry's hard work. Our realtor was shocked at closing! Barry was an advocate for us when other parties in the transaction had let us down.

We consider Barry a family friend now. He has walked alongside our family through good times and bad. I hope that you will read this book knowing that the author truly cares about his clients and seeks to provide them with what is best for them. I pray that Barry's expertise and talent blesses your family as it has mine.

Nicole Horsch
Author, *Sermon on the Mount of Messy*

Inspiration

As a mortgage professional for over twenty-four years, I have worked with and helped thousands of homeowners and clients. However, one client's story had a profound impact on me at an early stage in my career.

When I first started as a loan officer and learned how to do mortgage loans, my goal was to earn a decent living, and I accomplished that. I was a loan officer for about a year when I met this client who was referred to me by another customer of mine. "Joe" was not very hopeful when he first spoke with me. Having been turned down by few other lenders, he wasn't sure if I would be able to help him at all. Joe and his wife had some serious credit issues. They owed money to a lot of creditors because their daughter who was a special needs child, had a lot of health issues. His wife had decided to leave her job to care for their daughter and they were down to only one income. Things were fine for a while, but then Joe lost his job due to company layoffs. Joe's priority was to take care of his daughter and feed his family. He had to work odd jobs to earn a living, but he never gave up. To make ends meet, they used their credit cards to buy food and medicine for their daughter. After maxing out his credit cards and only working part time, he was not able to make payments on the cards. Most of them went to collection and they were hounded by debt collectors day and night. They threatened and abused him in attempts to collect their money, but you can't squeeze blood out of a turnip. He fell behind on his mortgage. His credit scores dropped to the low 500's. He was about to lose his home, and then by the grace of God, he found a full-time job that paid him a decent salary. His mortgage lender modified their mortgage and gave them a forbearance plan to get caught up on the mortgage. They also added all the money he owed from the missed mortgage payments to the back of the loan as a balloon payment. But at least he was able to keep the home and a roof over their heads.

He continued to work hard and paid his creditors as much as he could, but with the amount of debt he was under, he was finding no way out. Making minimum payments on those high-interest credit cards would take a lifetime to pay off. He had applied for a debt consolidation loan, but because of his low credit scores and a recent modification on his mortgage, he was unable to get a loan. Then, one day, he was prompted to call me by a friend of his, who had also been my previous client. He hesitated for few weeks, remembering how he was previously turned down by three other lenders.

When we first spoke, I did not judge him based on his credit scores. I did not tell him I couldn't help him, and I did not treat him like a number. I took the time to learn about his situation. I asked him about his family and found out about his daughter and her medical situation. I learned about him losing his job and all the whirlwind he had faced resulting from it. I told him that this was not going to be easy, but I would do everything I could to help him. I put together a plan to help him fix his credit by making payment arrangements with his creditors. I helped him settle some of his small credit card accounts, and I gave him a three-month plan which he followed exactly as I had laid out. Three months later, his credit scores went up to 628. He had now made twelve on-time payments on his mortgage, and I was able to help him refinance. We used the equity he had built in his home to settle and payoff $80,000 of his credit card debt and $40,000 in medical bills. The rate was a little higher but based on his credit and the situation he was in, it helped to clean up all his debt and give him a fresh start.

On the day of his loan closing, Joe and his wife broke into tears and told me I was a miracle worker. I was no miracle worker, I just took the time to learn his situation, helped him to fix the issues, and then closed his loan. But the satisfaction and the purpose that one loan gave me changed my entire career. It changed my perspective on things. I was no longer in it for the money. I was in it to help people. I helped thousands of homeowners get back on their feet. I helped many buy their first homes and while helping as many people as I could, I also made plenty of money. I just looked to help as many people as possible and God rewarded me.

There are too many people who come into this business with the idea of just making money. They do the wrong things. They take advantage of people and put them in bad loans so that they can turn a profit. Those people give this business a bad name. They do not belong in this business. Mortgage business done the right way is very satisfying and fulfilling but only if you take the right approach and do the right thing;

helping people, and providing solutions to their problems.

Being in the business as long as I have, you work with and help many clients on a day-to-day basis, but when you actually get to know your clients and work closely with them to help them solve their problems, it gives your job a new meaning and a purpose. When you look to help every client and treat them like they're your family member or close friend, it is no longer a job. It becomes a career full of passion and satisfaction.

Introduction

With more than twenty-four years in the mortgage business and finance industries, I have worked in many different capacities within the business. From a loan officer to a branch manager managing fourteen direct reports, an area manager responsible for 125 loan officers and loan processors, to a regional manager managing over forty offices in nine states for a large mortgage lender, I have recruited, hired, and trained hundreds of new loan officers. I have developed and promoted them to branch and area manager positions. Some of them are now running their own companies.

Although I have had a successful career, I was not born with a silver spoon in my mouth. I came from very humble beginnings. I have made plenty of money and have also lost money due to market conditions or my own mismanagement. Yet I have always made it back because I never took things for granted and never gave up. I worked hard and dedicated myself to serve my clients. I believe that hard work and dedication equals success.

I was born in Pakistan and came to the United States in 1989 when I was only twenty years old. Upon my arrival I only had $150.00 in my pocket. During my first week, I slept in a Sikh temple where I served food and swept the floors in exchange for meals and a place to sleep. My first job in the U.S. was selling books on a street corner in New York City. I had to work many odd jobs to make ends meet including working in delis and convenience stores. I worked in construction and drove a taxicab. Although I spoke English, I had an accent and I had to work hard to improve my English. I bought a small tape recorder and recorded myself, listening to myself and comparing myself to what I heard on radio, TV, and news. I worked hard to improve my language and accent. When I hear people making excuses for difficulties they have, I always share my story, because there is nothing you can't do if you work hard and take the initiative to better yourself.

My first job in the finance industry was working as a customer service representative for a credit card company. I was turned down for this job and many others because of not having experience. After being turned down for the job, I happened to read a local newspaper and saw their ad for the same position I was turned down for. It stated that they required no experience and were willing to train. So, I decided to write them a letter and point out that the ad said that no experience was necessary and that they were willing to train. I questioned them, "How do you know I can't do the job? Give me the opportunity and let me prove it to you." A few days later, I received a call from their HR manager who referred me to a temp agency, and they hired me as a temp. I worked hard at my new position and after four short months, I became their permanent employee. A few months later, I posted for a job in their collections department and got hired as a debt collector. I broke all kinds of production records and was soon promoted as a unit manager in charge of twelve debt collectors. In late 1998, I interviewed for a mortgage loan officer position and started my sales career in the mortgage industry. I was eager to learn, and like a sponge, began absorbing everything I could about the mortgage business and applied those skills to becoming one of the top loan officers in that office. As a loan officer, I aimed to not only do my own job well, but also to help everyone around me. I earned the respect of my peers, and this helped me get promoted to the branch manager position.

As a branch manager, I chose to take over a struggling branch and turned it into a successful, well producing branch. This got me promoted to the area manager position where I managed 125 loan officers in six branches. Within a year, I took the area sales from thirty-eight million a month to one–hundred million per month. Over the next three years our average production was over eighty-five million per month with the lowest delinquency and highest employee retention rate in the company. I was then promoted to a regional manager position where I was in charge of over 800 employees in forty branches across nine states. At the height of my career, I was making well over seven figures. And then came the biggest economic crisis this country has ever faced. Like many other Americans, I lost my job. The mortgage industry was in disarray, and it was hard to find a job in the industry.

I decided to purchase a retail business and paid over a million dollars for it, only to find out that the sellers had cooked the books to show fake profits. The business was rapidly losing money. Even after working as hard as I could, fourteen hours a day, seven days a week, I was unable to make it work. On top of that, I lost three family members over two years. I lost my mom due to cancer, and my youngest and oldest brother as well. Due to financial struggles, I started having problems in my marriage, which later ended in a divorce.

It was during these struggling times, I started drinking and questioning my faith. I was asking God, *Why me? What did I do to deserve this? Why am I going through these hard times and losing my loved ones?* Instead of thanking God for what I had, I was complaining about what I had lost. Then one day, I had the opportunity to serve at a homeless shelter where I got the answer to my question. I met few homeless people at the shelter who were very successful at some time in their lives. One was an electrical engineer, another a businessman; both had lost everything they had and ended up being homeless due to either drugs and alcohol or mental illness. I believe that God saved me that day. I got the answer to my question. No matter how tough things were, no matter how bad our financial situation was, we always had a roof over our heads, we always had food on the table, and we always had clothes on our backs. I was still able to provide for my family. I was still healthy. I fell to my knees that day and thanked God for everything we had. I thanked God that I was there to serve and not being served. That was the major turning point in my life. I came back to the mortgage business where I found my success. I worked hard and pulled myself out of the financial troubles I was in. I reconnected with my purpose and found new joy and satisfaction in helping people.

In every job I have had in my career, I did more than what was expected of me. I never took short cuts, I never cut corners. I always worked hard and went above and beyond. I also taught others what I had learned. I was eager to help other team members without expecting anything in return which earned me their respect. I was always looked at as one of the leaders.

I love the mortgage business because it has given me great satisfaction in helping others; customers and team members alike. It is deeply satisfying when I get to help clients dig out of massive debt after living paycheck to paycheck. I love when I get to help clients restructure and improve their financial situation and save money by paying off their high interest rate credit cards, payoff medical bills or collection accounts. In these moments, I feel like I am not only helping save them money, but also helping them restore their dignity. I've had clients break down in tears at loan closings because I assisted in a solution that was dramatically helping them out of desperate situations. In other situations, I have helped clients buy their first homes and accomplish their "American dream." I have helped clients buy multiple rental properties and build wealth. I wouldn't trade those experiences for anything. To this day, I work as a loan officer and a branch manager so I can help my clients and my staff change their lives for the better. I get repeat business and they refer me to their friends and family. It is a great feeling to know that you have made a difference in someone's life!

My new goal is to teach as many people as possible about the mortgage business and teach them the lessons I have learned. In the past twenty-four years I have seen every scenario play out in the business and know how to overcome it. I feel it is my responsibility to share that knowledge with other loan officers and homeowners alike and help them build wealth. Writing this book is my first step in that direction and I hope it makes a difference in others' lives.

In this short book, we will explore the possibilities of becoming a homeowner, whether you are buying your first home, or second, or third. We will also explore the strategies you can use to build wealth by refinancing and using the equity in your homes.

Concepts and strategies presented in this book are my experiences and the experiences of the clients I have helped during their wealth building process. This does not make it right or wrong advice. Just like any other investment, there are risks involved and you must evaluate those risks based on your own risk tolerance.

Why Should You Buy a Home?

There are many ways to build wealth. Some people save every penny to build and accumulate wealth. Some start a business to make money, while some work in high paying jobs. Some invest in the stock market, others in crypto currency. Bitcoin has made a lot of people rich these days. In my opinion, real estate is the safest investment that gives you a consistent rate of return if you are smart with your strategies, do your homework, and make good, calculated decisions.

In this book, we will explore the possibilities of building wealth by becoming a homeowner. You will also learn how to utilize your home and the equity built in it to further invest and build more wealth. Just like any other investment, the sooner you start, the more you will accumulate. But it is never too late to start.

In case you skipped over the introduction to this book, it is important to note that the concepts and strategies presented in this book are my experiences and the experiences of the clients I have helped during their wealth building process. This does not make it right or wrong advice. Just like any other investment, there are risks involved and you must evaluate those risks based on your own risk tolerance.

According to the studies, home values have increased fifteen percent over the last two years. Next year they are projected to increase at eight percent. The reason it is less is because of some fears about recession, but it is still a healthy increase. At the slowest pace, real estate still increases four percent every year. It is cyclical and goes up and down just like any other business. When the values go up too high, the market must correct itself. People cannot continue to buy homes at prices they cannot afford. So, prices do drop sometimes, but they always come back. In the crash of 2008 when home values dropped significantly, many people found themselves with little to no equity in their homes, even in negative equity in a lot of cases. But as the economy recovered, so did the home values.

Those same homeowners who had no equity and could not refinance or sell a few years ago, could now refinance their homes to lower their rates or to take cash out because home values have gone up again. In some areas, homes have almost doubled in value. There is also a shortage of homes in the U.S. and builders can't build homes fast enough. In addition, 4.8 million millennials turned age 30 in 2021 and that is an average age when people start buying homes. So, it is safe to assume that home values will always come back up.

When homes increase in value, you build equity. That equity can be used to build wealth in many ways. So, if you

If you are paying rent, you are paying someone else's mortgage, and therefore building someone else's wealth. Why not your own?

are not a homeowner yet, I suggest you become one sooner rather than later. Why?

For starters, if you are paying rent, you are paying someone else's mortgage, and therefore building someone else's wealth. Why not your own?

Let's look at some scenarios. These situations may vary because of several factors; including the market or area in which you are looking to buy, or the amount of property taxes and homeowner's insurance in those areas. New York and New Jersey are among some of the highest property tax areas. At the same time, you also have the opportunity to make more money in these areas because there are many high paying jobs available due to the demand in work force. Let's look at three scenarios in three different markets and see how to decide where to buy and how much you can afford.

Scenario 1:

Let's assume you are paying $2500 a month in rent for a one-to-two-bedroom apartment in Long Island, New York. When you apply for the rental apartment, they look at your credit to make sure you pay your bills on time. They also look at your income to make sure you earn two to three times the amount of the monthly rent you will be paying to make sure you can afford the rent and are not likely to default on your rent obligation. So, it is safe to assume you make $5000 -$7500 a month in income in this case. Why should you rent if you can buy your own home? The process of getting approved for a mortgage is similar for both options. The bank pulls your credit to make sure you pay your bills on time, and they check your income to make sure you can afford the payment on the loan you are applying for. So, if you must go thru the similar approval process to either rent or own, why not own? The only thing that could come in the way is not having enough savings for the down payment and closing costs to complete the purchase, but there are plenty of ways to come up with those funds. We will explore those options a little later in the book.

Average property taxes in Long Island are about $10,000 a year. Divide this number by twelve, and you will be paying approximately $833 per month in property taxes. The average homeowner's insurance is about $1800. Divide this by twelve and you get $150 per month.

Let's assume you are a first-time homebuyer and have good credit, (typically 720 or higher credit scores) and your income falls in line of the average income for the area. You can put as little as three percent down with a conventional loan. Your loan amount will be based off 97% of the purchase price. When you put less than 20% down payment you must pay PMI (private mortgage insurance.) We will cover the difference between (HOI) homeowner's insurance and (PMI) private mortgage insurance, later in this chapter. For now, in short, know that the HOI protects the homeowner (you), and PMI protects the lender in case of a loss. Based on a 720 credit score, you will be paying approximately $125 per month in PMI.

So, we start with the total housing payment of $2500 and deduct monthly taxes of $833, monthly HOI of $150 and monthly PMI of $125. This will leave us with the remaining $1392 for the payment for the loan. Assuming a 3.5% interest rate on a thirty-year loan, your total loan amount will be $309,991 which means your total purchase price will be $319,579. Instead of paying $2500 rent to someone else you can buy your own home and pay the same amount.

Scenario 2:

Now let's assume you live in or around New Jersey and your average property taxes are $7500 per year. Using the same $2500 per month in rent, this is how the numbers would work. $7500 divided by twelve = $625 per month in taxes, $150 per month for

HOI and $125 per month for PMI. This will leave you with $1600 for the loan payment. Using the same 3.5% interest rate over a thirty-year term, your loan amount will be $356,311 and the purchase price will be approximately $367,330. In other words, by purchasing in an area where taxes are less, you will be able to increase your purchase price.

Scenario 3:

Now let's assume you live in Virginia, North Carolina, Georgia, or other areas where property taxes are lower. For these areas, you may be looking around $3500 per year and possibly even lower in some areas. If you currently pay $2500 in rent, let's see how much house you can afford to buy. $3500 divided by twelve = $291.67, HOI of $150 and PMI of $152 will leave your remaining $1906.33 for the loan payment. Using the same 3.5% interest rate over a thirty-year term, your loan amount will be $424,530 and the purchase price will be approximately $437,660.

Even if your credit is average or less than perfect, you can still buy a home with only 3.5% down by using the FHA financing.

These numbers are just comparing $2500 in monthly rent with an estimated income of two times that amount (or $5,000 per month) assuming you don't have any other debts like car payments, credit card, or student loan payments, etc.

If you make more income or have more than one household income, you may qualify for a higher priced home, even in higher property tax areas. If you have other debts and want to know how much you qualify for, consult with an experienced loan officer.

(Note: Since writing the book and finally getting to publishing, the rates have risen significantly, so these numbers may vary. Please check with your loan officer to get accurate and up to date information.)

Credit Scores

If you have less than perfect credit or have had past credit problems, an experienced loan officer can also guide you as to how to fix those credit issues; helping you rebuild your credit and increase your credit scores so you can buy a home with a good interest rate. Your credit scores are calculated based on many different factors, including, how much debt you have, the number of accounts you have open, the kind of debt you have (auto loans, credit cards, student loans, etc.), the credit limits on those accounts, the balance you carry on those accounts, how you make your payments (whether you pay it in full, or make minimum payments every month, or more than the minimum payments), just to mention a few. All these things play a role in calculating your credit scores. Applying for a mortgage loan does not necessarily lower your credit score. Paying your accounts late or maxing out your credit limits will.

You can also use some available apps and websites like Credit Karma, Experian, and Freecreditreport.com to monitor your credit and check your credit progress. While these apps can be good to monitor your progress and keep an eye on your accounts, (even monitoring them to avoid any fraudulent activity), the credit scores calculated on these apps are based on a different credit model called the Vantage Scoring System. These scores can be thirty to sixty points off from the actual FICO scores which are used to lend mortgage and auto loans by the banks and other lenders. FICO scores are based on the Fair Isaac Scoring System. Many times, borrowers assume that the scores shown on these apps are their actual FICO scores and they get disappointed when the rates turn out to be different once the lender pulls their credit report with the FICO score. It's important to let the lender pull a credit report and know the actual scores so you can be provided with an accurate quote.

The Difference Between Homeowner's Insurance and Private Mortgage Insurance

Homeowner's insurance (HOI), also known as hazard insurance, protects the owner of the home in case of unforeseen circumstances and mishaps, such as a fire, a hurricane, wind or hail damage, water damage due to broken pipes and leaks, or a freak accident such as a car crashing into your home and causing damage. Homeowner's insurance protects you and covers damages. Insurance companies pay to either repair your home or rebuild it in case of a total loss. Assuming your premiums are paid accordingly, you will typically only be responsible for a small, predetermined deductible.

Private mortgage insurance (PMI), on the other hand, protects the lender against losses. If a buyer purchases a home and puts less than twenty percent as a down payment, the lenders take out an insurance from a third-party insurance provider to protect themselves in case the borrower defaults on their loan and stops making payments. If you put twenty percent or more as a down payment, then you are not required to pay for this insurance. This insurance is removed once you pay your loan down to eighty percent of the property value.

The only exception is if you have less than perfect credit, or if you go with an FHA loan. All FHA loans carry a mortgage insurance requirement regardless of the amount of down payment, in order to protect the agency against those losses. This insurance is called mortgage insurance premium (MIP), which is another name for PMI. You can remove this insurance by refinancing your home into a conventional loan once you improve your credit and either pay down the loan or build equity due to an increase in property value.

Down Payments and Closing Costs

Most people choose to rent because they do not have enough savings for the down payment and closing costs to buy a home. You need to have 3 − 3.5% for the down payment depending on the type of the loan and an additional 2-3% for the closing costs and prepaids. Prepaids are a portion of estimated property taxes and homeowner's insurance that lenders must set aside to pay when they become due. Typically, that is six months' worth. The lender will also collect future taxes and insurance with your monthly payments going forward. If you look at the scenarios we discussed previously, you'll notice that taxes and insurance were deducted from the $2500 payment. Some lenders may allow you to pay your own taxes and insurance outside of your monthly payment, but if you are a first-time home buyer and only putting the minimum allowed down payment, this option is not available. This is for more savvy borrowers who are disciplined and have experience with paying their own taxes and insurance. They also put twenty-five percent or more in down payments to be able to do that.

However, there are some ways you can buy a home with little or no money down. In times when the real estate market is slower, motivated sellers agree to pay either all, or part of your closing costs. That's called a seller credit. In that case you only need to come up with the down payment.

If you have parents or an immediate family member who is willing to give you a gift which does not require a repayment, it can be used for a down payment and or closing costs.

An experienced loan officer can run those numbers and let you know how much you are approved for and exactly how much funds you will need for down payment, closing costs, and prepaids and if there are options available for gifts and seller credits.

Zero Down Payment Assistance Programs

You can also buy your first home with a zero down payment loan. Many lenders have these programs and grants available to help first time home buyers purchase their first home with little or no money down. You can get up to 5% down payment assistance; of which 3–3.5% can go towards your down payment and 1.5% can go towards your closing costs and prepaids so you either need no money, or very little of your own funds to complete the purchase. The interest rates for these loans are usually a little higher but this is not a bad option since it allows you to buy a home with little to no out-of-pocket costs. Once you build some equity, you can always refinance your loan to get a lower interest rate in the future.

Compounding Interest Savings

Most people think that they need to come up with a twenty percent down payment in order to purchase their home. This statement is true if you are trying to avoid paying for PMI and have these funds in savings. Even most borrowers who have bought and sold homes before, think along these lines. Yet, consider this scenario. You are in your mid-to-late twenties or thirties, looking to buy a home and putting twenty percent down to avoid paying PMI, but you have no other account set up for your retirement.

You are purchasing a $350,000 home with a 20% down payment and a 3% interest rate.

Purchase Price	$350,000
20% Down Payment	$70,000
Loan Amount	$280,000
Monthly Payment	$1180.49
Total Interest Paid	$144,977
Home paid in	30 Years
Compounding Acct	$0
Retirement Income	$0

If all your focus would be to pay off your home and not have a mortgage payment, your home will be paid in thirty years, but you'll have no other savings for retirement.

Instead, consider the following scenario:

Purchase Price	$350,000
3% Down Payment	$10,500
$59,500 put in compounding account	

Loan Amount	$339,500
Monthly Payment	$1431.35 (slightly more)
Total Interest Paid	$175,784 (slightly more)
Home Paid in	30 Years

Compounding Acct	$650,675
	(balance after 30 years at 8% rate of return)

Retirement Income	$52,000 per year
	(based on 8% rate of return)

Most mutual funds over time have 8% rate of return. Even if you use half of that, it's not a bad retirement savings. Consult with your financial advisor to get a more accurate picture of your portfolio.

Tax Benefits

When you purchase a home, the interest on the mortgage loan is tax deductible unlike credit cards, auto loans, instalment loans, boat, or RV loans. Not only is the interest on the mortgage loan typically much lower than these unsecured loans, it is also tax deductible. The amount of tax deductibility is based on your income and the annual tax bracket you fall in. Please consult with your CPA or tax advisor to see how much interest you can write off.

Congratulations, if you have already bought your first home. You are already on your way to building wealth. And if you are on the fence thinking about it, take a leap of faith, and call an experienced loan officer in your area to help you with wealth building strategies.

When is a Good Time to Buy Real Estate?

Regardless of what's happening in the market, it is always a good time to buy real estate as long as the numbers work. You must be smart with your money. Pay attention to the area, and as you've heard realtors say, "location, location, location!" A home that needs some work in the best neighborhood, purchased at a lower price, then fixed over time will give you the best return on your investment.

To give you an example, I gave the same advice to two young men and suggested that they buy a home. One took my advice and bought a three-bedroom, two-bathroom home in a nice neighborhood for $400,000. His total mortgage payment is $2100 a month including taxes, insurance, and PMI. One of his friends decided to move in with him and is paying half of his mortgage. So, he gets to live in his own home and pays $1050 a month in monthly mortgage payment (his half). He is building equity in a market where home values are increasing fifteen percent a year. Two years later, his home could be worth over $500,000 and he could potentially build $100,000 in equity.

The other young man decided that the market was too crazy, and home prices were too high, and that he would wait and buy when the prices came back down. So, he decided to rent a small one-bedroom apartment for $2500 a month in rent plus utilities. If he waits two years for prices to come back down, (assuming they do go back down) he will have wasted $60,000 in rent with nothing to show. Do you think the home values will be low enough to have compensated for that loss? And even if home values go down, but the rates go up, that will bring your buying power down. So, my advice is, "don't wait to buy real estate, buy real estate and wait." You will build equity and wealth which can be multiplied and used to build even more wealth.

In June of 2017 I helped a client buy a home in Long Island, New York for $475,000 with FHA financing. The interest rate he qualified for at the time was 4.25%, he also had to pay $292 in PMI. His total payment was $3,658 which included his principal and interest, property taxes, homeowner's insurance, and PMI. In March 2021, less than four years later, his home appraised for $560,000 which is $85,000 higher. I helped him refinance his home with a conventional loan to lower his rate and remove PMI. His new rate was 3% and his new payment dropped to $3,027

> Don't wait to buy real estate. Buy real estate and wait.

per month. That is a savings of $631 per month. He built $85,000 equity or wealth in less than four years. That is 18% rate of return.

In 2021 and 2022, there were people willing to pay $30,000, $40,000, $50,000 and in some cases $100,000 over asking price to win a bid to buy a home. Now the home prices have started to level off, and in some cases, have come down a bit. Yet those same people are complaining about higher interest rates.

You see, you cannot buy a gallon of milk with the interest rate. Have you ever gone to a supermarket and bought a gallon of milk and paid for it with the interest rate? No. How do you pay for the milk? With the money. All the interest rate does is calculate the payment. If your income supports that payment and you can easily afford that payment, you should buy a home.

If you can buy a home for a cheaper price and you can afford the payment, don't let the higher interest rate stop you. You can always refinance in the future to lower the interest rate. There is a saying that goes, "marry the house and date the rate." I would add "divorce the rent" to that!

What Steps Should You Take as a First Time Buyer?

First time homebuyers are often unaware of how to prepare for their purchase. Others may be surprised to find out that they are already well-prepared to buy a home. If you are looking to buy your first home, the following steps will help you prepare to purchase your home successfully.

Establish Good Credit

You need to work on your credit and make sure you get your credit score as high as possible. Your monthly loan payment will be based on this interest rate, so make sure your credit is good. The better your credit score, the lower the interest rate you will get.

You need to open and establish two or three accounts, credit cards, or loans. Use these credit cards, but don't max them out. If your credit limit is $1,000, do not charge more than fifty percent of that amount. In other words, your balance should be lower than $500 on that card for your credit scores to remain high. When you start going up to 70, 80, or 90% of that limit, your scores will drop, especially if you max out that account or go over your credit limit. Then, your scores will take a major hit. Use these credit cards wisely to build credit, not to buy unnecessary things you cannot afford. Always make payments on time and pay more than the minimum monthly payments.

If you don't have any credit, ask your parents to add you as an authorized user on one of their accounts. This will give you the quickest way to start building credit. But do not use or abuse their account. You can end up harming their credit if you mishandle that account. Also, don't keep applying for credit if you were turned down. Wait and build your credit before applying for new accounts. Once you establish one or two accounts, keep using them and paying them off in full every month to show that you are credit worthy.

Save Money for Down Payment and Closing Costs

Next, you need to save enough money for the down payment and closing costs. You don't need a twenty percent down payment to buy a house. As a first-time buyer, you can pay 3-3.5% as a down payment. The closing costs are typically 2-4% of the loan amount depending on the area you live in. Having these funds in a savings account will help you negotiate the sales price. If you don't have these funds saved, there are still other ways to buy a home, but you would have to pay higher interest rates on your loan. Remember, there is nothing free in life, you either pay now or you pay more later. If you have the money for the down payment, but don't have enough for closing costs, you can ask the seller to help with the closing costs. Your realtor can help you negotiate those. Talk to a good loan officer and a good realtor. VA borrowers can buy a home with zero down payment. Similarly, if you buy in an area outside of a

> Remember, there is nothing free in life. You either pay now, or you pay more later.

heavily populated area, you could qualify for a USDA loan which also does not require any down payment. For those loans, you will need funds for the closing costs, unless you can get a seller credit. Even if you can get the seller credit towards closing costs, you should still have some money in the bank. It is typically recommended to have two to six months of mortgage payments in the bank. It shows the lender you have cash reserves, and you are a good credit risk for them. You will also ensure that you have funds in case of emergencies.

If you don't have enough funds, you can also buy your first home with a Down Payment Assistance (DPA) program offered by your local county, state, or a bank offered program. These grants and loans come with higher interest rates, but they allow you to purchase a home with little to no money down.

Your parents or an immediate family member such as a brother, sister, or children can also give you a gift towards your down payment and closing costs. This must be a gift and not a loan. As long as no repayment is required, you can use these funds for the down payment and closing costs. They would have to provide a proof of funds and sign a gift letter stating these funds are a gift and not a loan.

Have Stable Employment

You need to have a good, stable job. Lenders look at a two-year job history when considering you for a loan unless you just graduated from school and have your first job. In that case, you need to be at the same job for at least six months. Jumping from job to job does not show stability.

Gather Your Documents

These are typically the documents you need to get together when applying for a loan. Not all will apply to your situation, but your loan officer can let you know exactly what you would need.

1)   Most recent paycheck stubs covering thirty days of pay.
2)   W2 forms for most recent two years.
3)   Bank statements for two most recent months showing funds for down payment and closing costs.
4)   Copy of your government ID, driver's license, passport, etc.
5)   Copy of DD-214 (If you are a veteran, Current LES if active military.)
6)   Two most recent years of 1099 and federal tax returns (if self-employed).

Get Preapproved

Work with an experienced loan officer to get preapproved. They will guide you throughout the whole process to make sure there are no hiccups, and they will answer all your questions. They can also connect you to a good realtor if you don't have one yet.

Connect with a Good Realtor

Find a good realtor, someone who will fight for you and negotiate a good sales price and possibly get you some seller credit towards your closing costs. You do not pay for their services. Although they help you buy the home, their fees are paid by the seller.

Shop for Homes

When you have taken these steps, then you can begin to shop for homes and find your dream home. Once you find a home and the realtor helps you draw up the sales contract, your loan officer will start the loan process. It typically takes thirty to sixty days, depending on the market or area you are buying in, to close your loan.

Welcome to the homeownership! You have accomplished your "American dream." Enjoy your new home and make lots of good memories.

Building Wealth Through Home Ownership

Congratulations if you decided to buy your own home. It is a worthwhile investment. So, now that you are a homeowner, what can you do? How can you build wealth? In this last section, we will explore strategies to use the equity in your home to be put to good use and build wealth.

Every investor has a different risk tolerance. Some people are more conservative than others. Some are more aggressive and like to take risks, and some are in the middle. Those that take bigger risks often reap bigger rewards. But sometimes those bigger risks can also lead to losses. Homeownership is an investment. You must be a smart investor and manage your finances well to minimize those risks and maximize the rewards. Educate yourself. Learn, seek advice from an expert. Look for someone who knows the market and its ups and downs and is willing to give you sound advice. Stay away from those that are only looking to line their own pockets.

Let's talk about different options every homeowner has available and how to use the following strategies to their advantage.

Early Payoff

Perhaps you want to pay off your home as soon as possible so that you no longer have a mortgage payment. If this is your goal and priority you can accomplish this in several ways.

1) **Take a Shorter-Term Loan.** If your income allows you to qualify for a shorter-term loan like a ten, fifteen, or twenty-year loan, and you can afford that payment easily, you should consider that. You will pay less interest over the life of the loan, saving thousands of dollars in interest and you will be mortgage-free much sooner. If at the time of purchase, you didn't have enough income to qualify for a shorter-term loan, but

later you get a promotion, a pay increase, or have extra income from another source and now you can afford to pay a higher mortgage payment, then you could refinance into a shorter-term loan. Interest rates for shorter term loans are typically lower than the regular thirty-year mortgage, but there is cost involved. There are some fees you would have to pay to redo your loan, such as appraisal fees, title insurance, attorney fees, county recording fees, and in some counties, you must pay additional mortgage taxes and county fees. When refinancing, these fees can be financed in the new loan, so you don't have to pay them out of pocket. Many homeowners who have never refinanced before, think they must pay these fees out of pocket just like when they purchased the home, which is not the case. However, because these fees will be financed in your new loan, it will increase the balance of your mortgage. You must analyze and see if the benefit from refinancing outweighs the cost of the loan. Based on your savings, if you can recoup the cost of the loan within three to five years, and you plan to stay in your home for longer than that, it might be a good investment.

For example, if you initially got a $300,000 mortgage at 4% interest for thirty years with a principal & interest payment of $1432, you'll pay $215,608 in interest if you kept that same loan and never refinanced and never sold the home. If you refinance that mortgage on a fifteen-year term at a 3.25% interest rate and you had to pay $10,000 in fees to do that, you will pay a total of $82,089 in interest. That's $133,518 in savings. This would be a great return on your investment. Keep in mind that because the term is shorter, your overall monthly payment will be $746 higher in this case. The only way that will make sense to do is if you have more income and you can easily afford to make that payment without putting an extra burden on yourself.

2) **Pay Extra towards Principal.** If the rate on the shorter term is not low enough and you don't want to pay the cost to redo the loan because the cost is excessive, you do not need to refinance, in order to pay that home off sooner. You can just increase your monthly mortgage payment. Anything you pay extra, ask the lender to apply those payments towards the principal. By doing this, you can reduce the term of your mortgage. Extra payments will

reduce the principal balance; therefore you will pay less interest over the life of the loan.

How much extra you should pay? It depends on how much you can afford. Typically, if you can make one extra payment a year, depending on your loan balance and interest rate, you can cut the term of your loan by four to six years. With a $300,000 loan amount at 3% interest, the 30-year payment would be $1264.81. If you just made one extra payment a year, you could reduce the term of the loan down to 26.44 years and you won't have to pay any cost to refinance that loan. There are three easy ways to accomplish this:

i) **Make one extra payment a year.** Usually, people do this when they get their tax refund. As soon as they get their refund, they send in a check for one extra payment and ask the lender to apply those funds to the principal.

ii) **Take your monthly payment and divide it by twelve. Add that amount to your monthly payment and pay that every month.** For example, if your monthly payment is $1264, divide that by twelve and you would get $105.33. $1264.00 +105.33= $1369.33. Pay this amount every month and you can accomplish the same thing.

iii) **Make biweekly payments.** When you make biweekly payments, you will pay half of your monthly mortgage payment every two weeks. $1264 divided by two = $632, (paid every 2 weeks). By doing this, you will make one extra payment each year. When you pay biweekly, you will make 26 payments of half of your regular payments, instead of twelve full payments. Twenty-six divided by two is thirteen total payments. So instead of paying monthly and making twelve payments a year, you just made an extra payment without changing your monthly budget.

Keep in mind that some lenders don't accept biweekly payments. In that case, use one of the other options. Another thing to keep in mind when paying biweekly, is that those payment dates will fall on different pay periods that may not coincide with your pay dates, so you want to make sure you budget this properly.

Cash Out Refinance

The equity you build in your home is your most powerful tool. You can use this equity to accomplish many things, including building wealth. Here are some reasons why you would want to cash out your equity.

You bought your home five years ago. You have been making extra payments towards the principal. The home increased in value 8-15% every year over the last five years. You have built a considerable amount of equity in your home. If you bought the home for $350,000 five years ago, your home is now worth $450,000. You built $100,000 equity in five years. This is your money, your savings, your wealth. You could not possibly save that amount of money if you were renting. You'd be paying someone else's' mortgage.

You can cash out up to 80% of your home's value. In this case, that would be $360,000. Assuming you only put a three percent down payment when you bought the home, and you have been sending extra payments, your estimated balance is now $300,000. You can take out $60,000 cash out from your home's equity. You will still have twenty percent remaining equity in your home, so if you decide to sell you will still walk away with twenty percent. What could you do with the $60,000? How can you use it to build more wealth?

You could not possibly save that amount of money if you were renting. You'd be paying someone else's mortgage.

Home Improvements

You could repair or get a new roof. You could remodel a kitchen or a bathroom. You could install a pool or a purchase a hot tub. Build a new driveway. Put up a new fence, or all of the above. The interest on the new loan will be a lot less than if you borrowed money on a credit card or an installment loan; even less than a second mortgage or a home equity loan.

Make a Major Purchase

You can use this money to make a major purchase. You can buy a car, truck, or a boat. A tractor perhaps? A Harley Davidson? Or pay for a major surgery? The interest you will pay on the mortgage loan will not only be lower than the interest on these loans, it may also be tax deductible. Please check with your tax advisor to see which tax deductions you may quality for on a yearly basis.

Pay for College Education

You can take out the cash and put it in a college fund to pay for your children's college education. Instead of your children taking on student loans, they can graduate college without any debt. Or, if you have your own student loans that have been accruing interest and you have not been able to pay them off, you can now pay off those past student loans and get them off your back. I have seen those student loans ruin people's credit due to payments being deferred and interest continually accruing; they end up owing more on those loans than the amount initially borrowed. This also lowers your credit scores. By paying those loans off, you get them off your credit and can increase your credit score again.

Compound and Save for Retirement

If you have not been putting money away for your retirement, it's not too late. You can start now. You can also use this money to start a retirement fund. Most mutual funds have an eight percent rate of return over time. Even if we use half of that, $60,000 invested over twenty-five years at a four percent rate of return, you will accumulate $162,825 in your retirement account. Consult with a certified financial advisor for advice on investment in stocks, bonds, or mutual funds.

Debt Consolidation

You can pay off high interest rate credit cards and installment loans. In doing so, you can also lower your monthly expenses and increase your cash flow. Using this option correctly can have a phenomenal impact on your financial success. Once you consolidate your bills, you want to make sure that you don't go back and reuse those unsecured debts because that could get you in trouble. If you are using credit cards wisely and paying off the balance in full every month, and you are earning points and airline mileage, that's a great use of credit cards. But if you are using credit cards to get instant gratification and to buy things when you didn't have the means to pay for them in cash, and then paying just the minimum payments each month, you may soon find yourself living from paycheck to paycheck. If you find yourself in this situation, a debt consolidation loan, or a debt restructure loan can work for you. Let's look at an example and find out how these numbers work out to your benefit.

Let's say that you have a mortgage balance of $300,000 and you are currently paying 3.00% interest on a thirty-year mortgage. Your current principal and interest payment is $1475 per month. But you also have credit cards at high interest rates, installment loans, and student loans. Typically, these credit cards have an average interest rate of 18 -21%. The department store cards have even higher interest rates of 21% up to 32%. When you make just the minimum required payment on these cards, the majority, if not all, of this payment, goes towards paying the interest and very little, if any, goes towards paying down the principal balance. Making minimum payments on a credit card will take you a very long time to payoff credit cards. Making minimum payments also lowers your credit scores. You must pay a lot more than the minimum payments in order to pay these cards off. Let's add these bills and see what your current financial situation looks like now. Keep in mind, monthly payments shown on the next page are minimum monthly payments only.

Creditors	Interest Rate	Current Balances	Monthly Payments
Current Mortgage	3.00%	$300,000	$1475
Credit Card 1	18.00%	$10,000	$350
Credit Card 2	18.00%	$8,000	$260
Credit Card 3	14.00%	$7,000	$220
Installment Loan	6.00%	$5,000	$190
Student Loan	8.00%	$12,000	$60
TOTAL		**$342,000**	**$2,555**

If you took out a new loan for $360,000 as a cash out refinance, at a five percent interest rate, your new payment on a twenty-five-year loan will be $2104 per month. After paying off the $300,000 previous mortgage, $42,000 of the above-mentioned debt, assuming your cost is about $8,000 to do the loan, you can still walk away with $10,000 cash in your hands. Which you can use to do home improvements, take a vacation, invest in stocks, or just put it in your savings account as a nest egg. Right now, you pay $2,555 a month. With this refinance, your new mortgage payment will be $2,104 which will lower your monthly expenses by $451. That's $451 in extra cash flow that can be used to make purchases in cash going forward, as opposed to using credit cards. That $451 can be used to put money away in an IRA account for your retirement. Or, that $451 that can be used to purchase life insurance to protect your family and loved ones. Right now, you are throwing that money away and paying high interest rates on those credit cards. The refinance option puts you in a much better financial situation going forward. Even if your interest rate on the mortgage went up by 2.00%, your cash in hand went up by $451 a month. And the $8,000 financed in the loan that paid your cost for doing the loan can be recouped in 17.74 months. This makes it a great investment for a hefty return.

Remember, when you go to the grocery store to buy a gallon of milk, you don't pay for it with interest, you pay for it in dollars. And if this loan can save you $451 a month, how many gallons of milk can this money buy you? A whole lot.

Remember the following key points to apply when you do a debt restructure. It is important to use this to your advantage and not to get further in debt.

1)   Don't use credit cards anymore. Use this extra cash flow to buy things with cash.

Barry Sharif

2) Put all, or some of this money in a savings account for future use.

3) Buy life insurance to protect your family and loved ones.

4) Invest some of it in an IRA account on monthly basis. $451 invested in an IRA and/or mutual funds at a very nominal four percent rate of return over twenty-five years will turn this into $231,872 savings with compounding interest. By the time you pay off your home in twenty-five years, you'll have these retirement savings along the way. As always, it is best to consult with a financial advisor for stock and mutual funds advice to verify these numbers as they would apply to you personally.

5) You can also pay this $451 towards your new mortgage payment as an extra principal payment. By doing that you can reduce the term of your new mortgage. Paying $451 extra every month will pay your new loan off in 17.73 years and you will cut 7.27 years off your mortgage. This will save you $183,552 in interest.

Buy an Investment Property or Multiple Properties

Let's assume you refinanced your primary home and took $60,000 cash out. You can use this cash as a down payment and for closing costs to purchase another property as an investment. When buying an investment property, you need to put twenty to twenty-five percent in down payment. A $250,000 investment home will require a $50,000 down payment and $10,000 in closing costs and prepaids. The remaining $200,000 financed at a seven percent interest rate over thirty years will have a principal and interest payment of $1,330.60. You will also pay approximately $300.00 in estimated taxes and $125.00 in estimated home insurance, which will make your total payment $1,755.60. If you rent that home for $2,200 per month. someone else (a tenant) is now paying your mortgage on this investment property. After paying your mortgage, you will have net rental income of $444 per month. Invest this $444/month in mutual funds and let it compound interest. $444/month, over thirty years at a four percent rate of return can end up in a $308,157 retirement savings.

Next, wait five years and let this investment property appreciate in value, then refinance it to get cash out to purchase another investment property. If you renovate the property and upgrade it prior to renting it, you can rent it for more money. Repeat the steps mentioned above and set up another compounding account. Imagine how much wealth you can create. You can repeat this over and over and continue to build a massive real estate portfolio. This strategy is also called the BRRRR strategy.

Buy – Renovate – Rent – Refinance to get Cash Out – Repeat

Buy – Renovate – Rent – Refinance to get Cash Out – Repeat

The mortgages on these properties will be paid by your tenants. You will continue to invest the net rental income in compounding accounts to build wealth.

Multi–Unit Properties

When you buy a multi–unit property, the rental income generated from the other units also gets used as income to qualify you for the loan. For example, if a two–unit home generates $1500+$1500 = $3,000 in rent. 75% of that, or $2,250 is used as qualifying income. If the total mortgage payment is equal to or less than $2,250, you can purchase that property. All you need is the down payment and closing costs.

Do you remember the initial investment you had to make in the very first home you purchased? It was just 3-6%. (3-3.5% in down payment and rest in closing costs and prepaids.) You just have to get started with your first home. Prepare, talk to a qualified mortgage professional in your area and get prequalified. Ask for advice, take a leap of faith, and begin your journey to wealth and prosperity.

Reverse Mortgage

It would be a disservice and a missed opportunity if we didn't talk about reverse mortgages. This product has a lot of advantages for senior citizens.

There are about 10,000 people turning the age of 65 or older every single day. So, it is important that we understand how this product works. What's new? What are the advantages? And how are people using them?

Before I get into details of this product, I'd like to share a story of an elderly couple I knew. Both the husband and the wife were in their 70's. The wife had heart problems and also suffered from a stroke. She was unable to function. The husband was taking care of her. Being retired, they were on social security fixed income. They had a ton of medical bills that were not covered by the Medicare. Their children were grown and lived in other states with their own families. This couple had worked hard all their lives to pay off their home, which they wanted to leave for their children. They raised their children with love and provided them with a good education. Unfortunately, those children now lived with their own families in other states and didn't have time to care for their elderly parents. It is a harsh reality, and a sad one. So, what are those elderly parents supposed to do?

I was able to help them get a reverse mortgage. They paid off all their medical bills and credit cards. They received $100,000 in cash out which they put away as a nest egg for any future needs. They also received a line of credit which if they don't use will grow and earn them interest. It's there if they need any additional funds in the future, and they will never have to make another mortgage payment as long as they stay at that property. Not to mention, they will get to live in the comfort of their own home, as opposed to a nursing home. Knowing that I helped them make their lives better is the greatest satisfaction I get out of this career.

What is a Reverse Mortgage?

This product was created in the 1980's to help homeowners, 62 years and older, convert part of the equity in their home into money that can be used during retirement. Recent changes to the program have made it a more effective way for eligible homeowners to gain financial flexibility while maintaining ownership of their home.

Financial research coming out of prominent universities demonstrates how a reverse mortgage may extend the life of a retiree's nest egg, and significantly increase the likelihood that they will have enough money longer into their retirement. A reverse mortgage allows the borrower to access some of the equity built up in their home and convert it into cash or a credit line. It can also be used to finance the purchase of a home that better fits their needs.

Monthly mortgage payments are not required. The borrower is still responsible for the property taxes, insurance, and maintenance, just as a traditional home loan. As long as they meet these obligations, the loan balance does not become due until the last remaining homeowner no longer uses the home as a primary residence, or the home is sold.

The loan amount they qualify for is calculated based on several factors, including:

- The age of the youngest borrower
- The appraisal value of the home

- The loan options they choose
- The prevailing market interest rates

Eligible property types include single family homes, 2-to-4-unit properties as long as the borrower occupies one of the units as their primary residence, condos and townhomes (must be FHA Approved), and manufactured homes (built after June 1976, titled and taxed as real property under state laws).

All borrowers on the loan must be at least 62 years old, and the home must be used as their primary residence and must have sufficient equity. The borrowers must receive reverse mortgage counseling from an independent counselor who is approved by the U.S. department of Housing and Urban Development (HUD). Reverse mortgage loans known as Home Equity Conversion Mortgages, or HECMs are insured by the Federal Housing Administration.

What are the Advantages of a Reverse Mortgage?

There are no monthly mortgage payments required on reverse mortgage loans as long as the borrower complies with their loan agreement and lives in the home. If they have an existing mortgage and other debts, and substantial home equity, they can use the reverse mortgage to consolidate those debts to reduce their monthly expenses.

They can get additional cash back for other needs such as home improvements, medical bills, etc., and there are no monthly payments required.

The borrower retains complete ownership of their home. The proceeds they receive from a reverse mortgage are generally not considered taxable income. (Always consult a qualified tax advisor for tax questions or advice.)

A reverse mortgage could help delay receiving Social Security benefits. The longer they wait to access Social Security, the more they will receive when they do.

A reverse mortgage can also be used to make their retirement savings last longer. It replaces a traditional mortgage to eliminate monthly mortgage payments.

The borrowers have a choice on how they receive their funds from a reverse mortgage. They can get a lump sum payout to buy another home, pay off debts, payoff medical bills, etc. They can also supplement their retirement income by receiving a payment each month either for a set period, or as long as they live in their home. They can also get their funds as a line of credit. The interest is only charged when the proceeds are taken. If the line is not used, they actually receive interest. Interest compounds and they can accumulate this as additional retirement funds that can be used later. Or they can use a combination of these options.

When Does it Have to be Repaid?

A reverse mortgage is for a primary residence only. If the homeowner decides to move out of the home and it is no longer their primary residence, the lender will require you to pay off the loan.

- The borrower decides to sell the home. Once the home, is sold the mortgage must be paid.

- The borrower or borrowers pass away, the mortgage must be paid.

- Borrowers can also refinance their Reverse mortgage into a forward mortgage if they choose to do so.

There is big misconception or a myth that if you get a reverse mortgage, the lender will take your home away from you, or they will keep the house. Lenders make money from earning the interest on the loan; they are not interested in managing the properties. It costs them money to manage the property. That's why in most cases of defaults, a lender rather modifies the loan and let the homeowner stay in it rather than foreclose on it. If they foreclose, they never get all their money back. In the case of a foreclosure, the lender takes a major loss.

In the case of a borrower's death their heirs have three options:

1)   If there is equity in the home, they can sell the home and payoff the loan. Remaining proceeds go to the heirs.

2)   If they love the home and want to keep it, they can pay off the loan and keep the home. If they don't have cash to pay off the loan, they can take a loan in their own name and pay off the loan. In some cases where the home has equity, one of the heirs buys the home in their name and pays off the other heirs' proportionate share(s).

3)   If there is no equity, and the money owed on the home is more than the home is worth, heirs can choose to walk away and turn the home to the lender and let the lender deal with it. In this case, the lender will most likely lose money, but the loan is insured by the Federal Housing Administration which means the lender will get their money back and FHA will end up taking the loss. That's why they have mortgage insurance on the loan to protect them in case of a loss.

By the way, those are the same three options if they have a regular forward mortgage. So, in case of their death, a reverse mortgage is no different than the regular mortgage. The only difference is that on the regular mortgage you make payments to pay down the loan. Over time, the balance decreases and the loan gets paid off. On the reverse mortgage, you don't have to make a payment. The interest is paid from the equity of the home, therefore the balance goes up rather than down. The lender gets paid upon the borrower's death as outlined above.

The borrower also has the option to make payments if they so choose and can afford to make them. If they make regular payments towards the interest, the balance of the loan does not increase.

You can call an expert reverse mortgage loan officer in your area to explore your individual needs.

ABOUT THE AUTHOR: BARRY SHARIF

Barry offers an extensive background in finance and mortgages. Beginning in 1996, he started his finance career in the credit card division for HSBC in Virginia. Diligently working his way up, he eventually transitioned over to a large national mortgage company in New York where he worked in many roles starting from a loan officer to branch manager, area manager, and finally to a regional manager, where he oversaw forty-three branches in nine states.

This experience has allowed him to see the industry from nearly every perspective possible: loan officer, underwriter, executive positions, and as a mortgage trainer. He has trained thousands of loan officer throughout his career.

"I am very passionate about what I do. I genuinely care about my clients, and I always put myself in their shoes. I ask myself this question, *if this was my family member would I do this loan for him or her?* If my answer is yes, I wholeheartedly present the solution. I am not a pushy 'in your face' salesperson. I give my customers different options that fit their needs and I let them pick and choose what is ideal for them. I give my expert opinion, but at the end of the day, it needs to be the loan that fits their needs."

When not at work, Barry loves to spend time with his wife and their five children. He loves their pet dog Knight, and their cat, Venus. His family believes in giving back to the community and they serve as volunteers at a local homeless shelter.

Connect with Barry online at www.barrysharif.com

With Sharif Consulting, Barry's mission is to share and transfer his knowledge to other loan officers and educate them with these concepts. The company offers a variety of classes and levels of training, including: Loan Officer Sales Training to those who are looking to join the business or have been in the business for less than a year and never received any formal training from their employers. Advance Sales Mastery Training is available to loan officers who have been in the business for more than a year and are looking to increase sales and take their careers to the next level. He also offers Mortgage Sales Manager Training to new managers and experienced loan officers who are looking to become managers and manage their own teams. Additional courses include recruiting, interviewing, pipeline management, how to motivate and inspire your teams, and time management classes. Barry's company also offers these services to other mortgage companies who are looking to provide these training courses to their sales force.

To learn more, visit www.sharifconsulting.com or www.barrysharif.com

Additional copies of this book may be
purchased
on Amazon.com
and BarnesandNoble.com

.